Famous Lives

The Life of
Clara Barton

By Kathleen Connors

Gareth Stevens
Publishing

GS

SOCIAL
STUDIES

Please visit our website, www.garethstevens.com. For a free color catalog of all our high-quality books, call toll free 1-800-542-2595 or fax 1-877-542-2596.

Library of Congress Cataloging-in-Publication Data

Connors, Kathleen.
The Life of Clara Barton / by Kathleen Connors.
 p. cm. — (Famous lives)
Includes index.
ISBN 978-1-4824-0378-7 (pbk.)
ISBN 978-1-4824-0379-4 (6-pack)
ISBN 978-1-4824-0375-6 (library binding)
1. Barton, Clara, — 1821-1912 – Juvenile literature. 2. American Red Cross — Biography — Juvenile literature. 3. Nurses — United States — Biography — Juvenile literature. I. Connors, Kathleen. II. Title.
HV569.B3 C66 2014
361.7634—dc23

First Edition

Published in 2014 by
Gareth Stevens Publishing
111 East 14th Street, Suite 349
New York, NY 10003

Copyright © 2014 Gareth Stevens Publishing

Designer: Nick Domiano
Editor: Kristen Rajczak

Photo credits: Cover, pp. 1, 13 Buyenlarge/Archive Photos/Getty Images; p. 5 Photo Researchers/ Photo Researchers/Getty Images; p. 7 Photos.com/Thinkstock.com; p. 9 Fotosearch/Archive Photos/ Getty Images; p. 11 Popperfoto/Popperfoto/Getty Images; p. 15 FPG/Hulton Archive/Getty Images; p. 17 DEA/G. DAGLI ORTI/De Agostini Picture Library/Getty Images; p. 19 Hulton Archive/Hulton Archive/Getty Images; p. 21 New York Public Library/Photo Researchers/Getty Images.

Printed in the United States of America

CPSIA compliance information: Batch #CW14GS: For further information contact Gareth Stevens, New York, New York at 1-800-542-2595.

Contents

Boldface words appear in the glossary.

Angel of Service

Clara Barton spent her life helping others. She was called the "angel of the battlefield" because of her great service during the **Civil War**. Clara's work is still important today—she founded the American Red Cross!

5

Clara was born Clarissa Harlow Barton in 1821. Her birthday was Christmas day! Clara lived with her parents, two older sisters, and two older brothers in Oxford, Massachusetts.

7

Early Work

Clara began teaching at 15. In 1852, she opened a school in New Jersey. Though she made the school a success, the next year they put a man in charge. Clara left to work in Washington, DC.

9

War Breaks Out

When the Civil War began in 1861, Clara **volunteered** right away! At first, she worked at hospitals in Washington, DC. She also gathered supplies such as food, clothing, and **medicine**.

11

Soon, Clara was on the battlefield! She worked in field hospitals helping **wounded** soldiers. As the war continued, she traveled with the army. She **organized** the medical supplies and found missing soldiers.

13

The Red Cross

Clara went to Europe after the war ended. There, she met with the International Red Cross, a group that helps people affected by war. They had heard about her great work on the battlefield.

15

Clara and the International Red Cross worked for better conditions for **prisoners of war**. They wanted wounded or sick soldiers to be allowed care during wartime. Many countries signed an agreement stating these ideas.

17

In 1881, Clara founded the American Association of the Red Cross. It would offer **relief** during war and in other times of need. In 1889, Clara and the Red Cross helped the people of Johnstown, Pennsylvania, after a flood.

19

Remembered Today

Clara worked in the field with the Red Cross until she was 77 years old! She died at age 91 on April 12, 1912. Her work lives on in the good the Red Cross still does today.

Timeline

1821——Clara is born.

1852——Clara founds a school.

1861– —Clara volunteers during the Civil
1865   War.

1881——Clara founds the American Red
     Cross.

1912——Clara dies at age 91.

Glossary

Civil War: a war in the United States between the Northern and Southern states

medicine: a drug taken to make a sick person well

organize: to put together in an orderly way

prisoner of war: a soldier held against their will during wartime

relief: assistance, especially during times of war or great need

volunteer: to work without pay

wounded: hurt

For More Information

Books

Edison, Erin. *Clara Barton*. North Mankato, MN: Capstone Press, 2013.

Harkins, Susan Sales, and William H. Harkins. *The Life and Times of Clara Barton*. Hockessin, DE: Mitchell Lane Publishers, 2009.

Websites

American Red Cross: Founder Clara Barton
www.redcross.org/about-us/history/clara-barton
Read about the founding of the American Red Cross.

Clara Barton National Historic Site
www.nps.gov/clba/index.htm
Find out more about the historic site in Maryland devoted to Clara Barton.

Index